Follow Me
To
Distance Learning

Fulton Books, Inc.
Meadville, PA

Published by Fulton Books 2021

ISBN 978-1-63710-395-1 (paperback)
ISBN 978-1-63710-396-8 (digital)

Printed in the United States of America

Follow Me
To
Distance Learning

Written by

Agnieszka Petlik

Illustrated by

Natalia Ramirez

I open my eyes and see,

There is a new world in front of me.

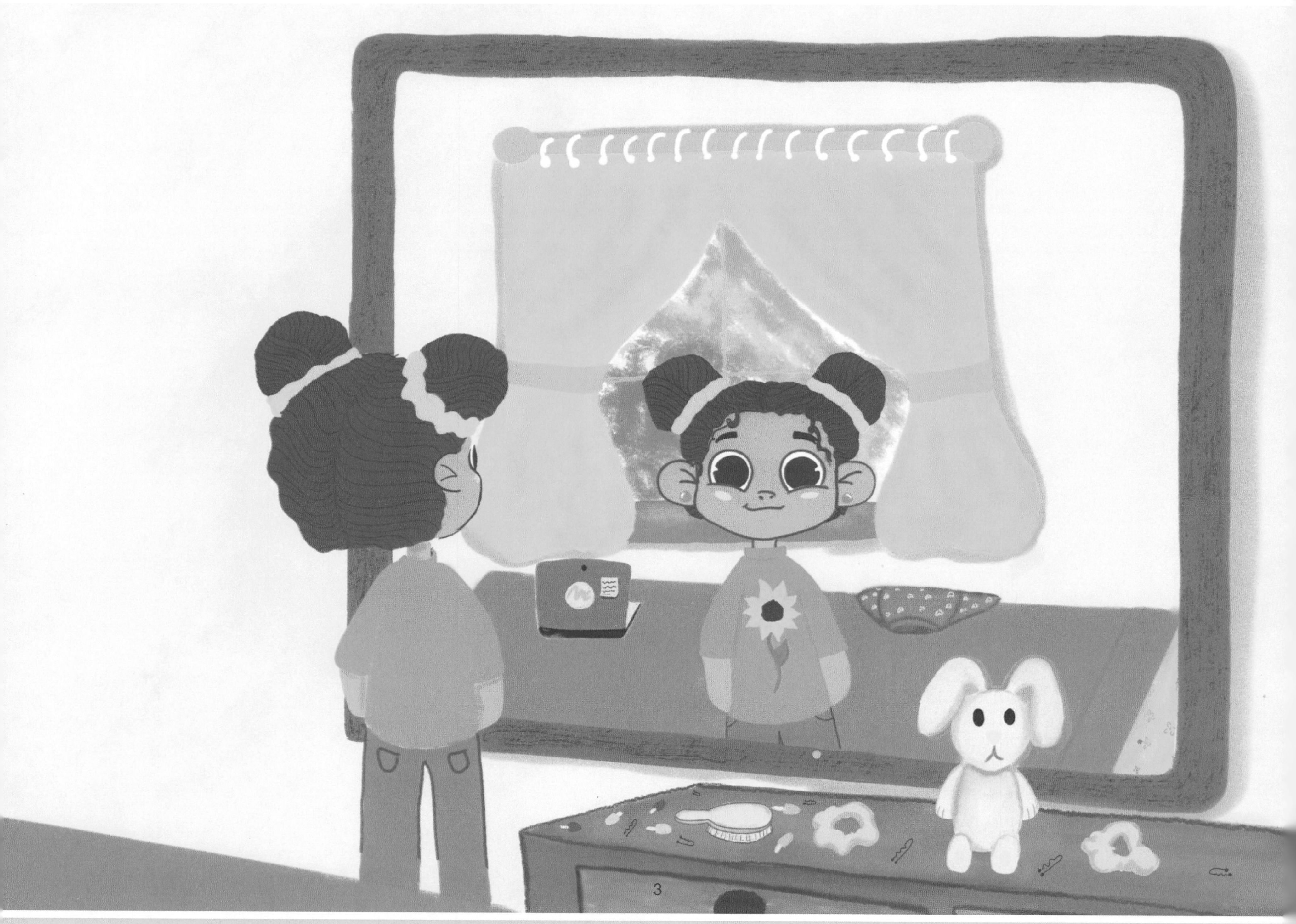

I get dressed and brush my hair,

Wondering what will we be working on over there.

I click the button and sit in my chair.

We all mute and try not to stare.

__ ad

__ itten

__ cissors

m s h m e

I see faces in boxes all in a row.

How interesting to be in such a school show.

I raise my hand and smile big.

My teacher calls my name while doing this gig.

I'm nervous and excited all at once to say,

"Dear teacher, I don't want to do distance learning. I just want to play."

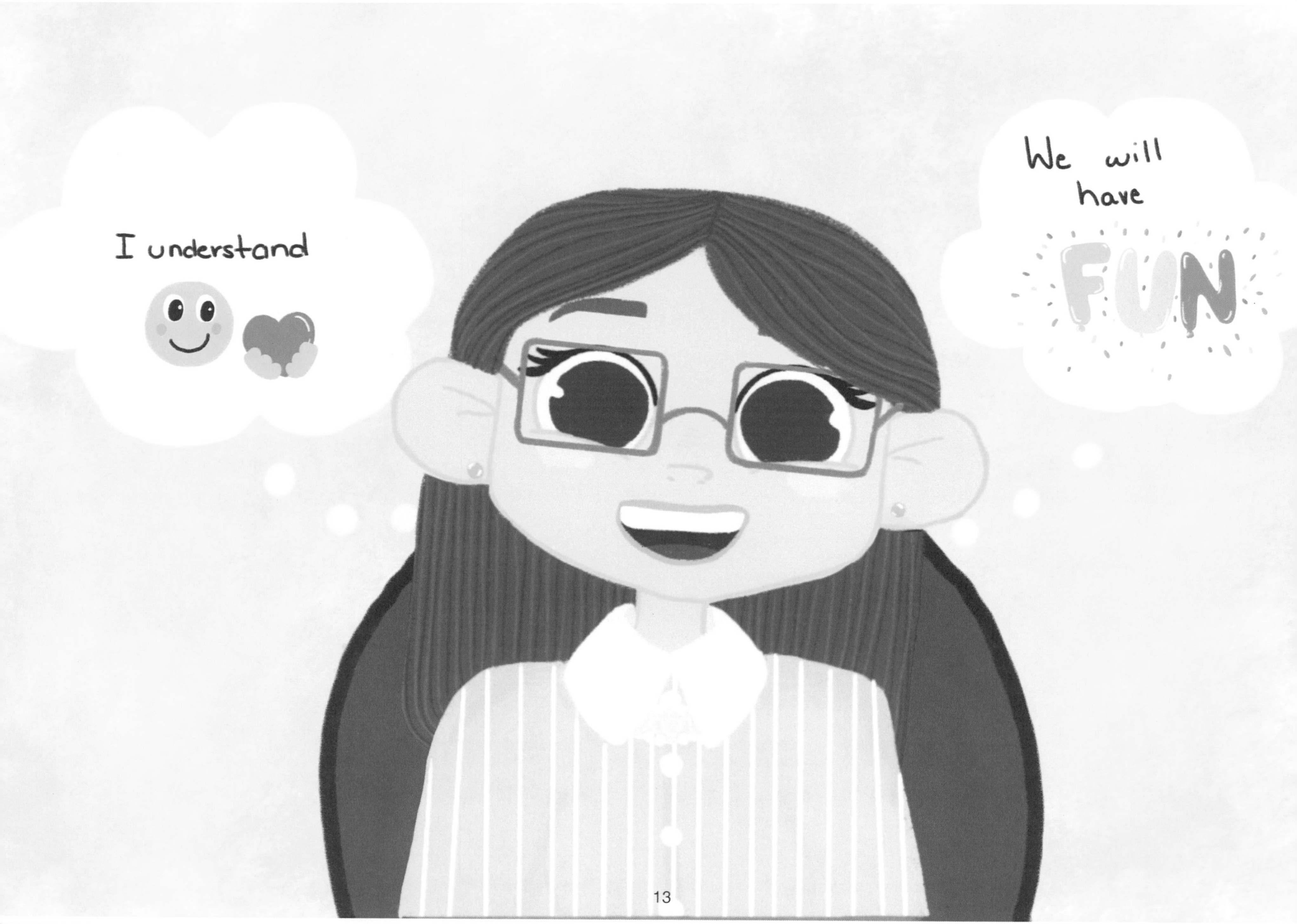
I understand
We will have
FUN

She smiles big with empathy and care,

Knowing all too well that this was not fair.

We are all in this together,

We will have fun,

Just give it a chance and don't try to run.

I miss classroom friends and the hallways in school. But maybe this computer will teach me something cool. And with a click of a mouse and a new seesaw game, I get engaged even though things weren't the same.

I start to learn reading, writing, and math.

Such a different way to start on this path.

Breakout rooms are my new favorite time,

For my friends and I get to tell jokes and play with slime.

I notice, my teacher is proud of me,

Her face beams with pride.

I'm glad I went along for this new ride.

So whenever things get hard, and you're feeling blue.

Remember that your teachers, friends, and family will see you through!

Check Your Understanding!

1-What is the problem at the heart of this story?

2-How does this problem exist in the real world?

3-How do the characters' feelings change throughout the story?

4-What lesson did the character learn?

First
Next
Then
After
Finally

About the Author

Agnieszka Petlik came from Poland in 1991 with her parents and two brothers. As a young child, Ms. Petlik was inspired by teachers in her school and vowed to be an educator one day. Her father, Henryk, valued education and always empowered her to continue her learning. Today, Ms. Petlik is a grade 1 distance learning teacher for Simsbury Public Schools in Connecticut. She has been in the education field for over eight years and served in districts such as New Britain and Plainville. Ms. Petlik has taught regular education students and special education students, where diversity and needs vary. She currently is a doctorate student at Central Connecticut State University with a dissertation focus on equity in distance learning. Ms. Petlik's experiences as a teacher and a parent of her ten-year-old daughter Natalia have motivated her to write this book. *Follow Me to Distance Learning* is a dedication to all the children, teachers, and families who have been impacted by COVID-19 and are balancing distance learning and life.

CPSIA information can be obtained
at www.ICGtesting.com
Printed in the USA
BVRC090002030621
608682BV00024B/40